CW00832329

EXAM-BUSTING TIPS

HOW TO PASS EXAMS
THE EASY WAY

summersdale

EXAM-BUSTING TIPS: HOW TO PASS EXAMS THE EASY WAY

Copyright © Summersdale Publishers Ltd 2005

Text by Nick 'BA Hons' Atkinson

Illustrations by Rob '3 A Levels' Smith

Summersdale Publishers Ltd
46 West Street
Chichester
West Sussex
PO19 1RP
UK

www.summersdale.com

Printed and bound in Great Britain

ISBN 1 84024 076 8

EXAM-BUSTING TIPS

CONTENTS

Introduction

For many people, sitting exams represents all that is daunting in the world of academia. The months, weeks, days or minutes of revision that you have put in, probably with a degree of reluctance, all build up to the horror that is the day of the exam.

But help is at hand.

If you dread the impatient shuffling outside the exam hall while you wait to be called in, relax. If you fear being suffocated by people claiming to be either 'terrified', 'on the verge of a nervous breakdown' or, in particularly irritating instances, 'absolutely ready for any topic that should arise', breathe easy. And if you have ever been known to go into an exam with only one pen, then don't panic, my under-equipped friend – all is by no means lost.

You too can be part of the elite group of people who regularly bask in post-exam glory.

Strength of mind

FOOD FOR THOUGHT

During the exam period, it is imperative that you eat well and consume lots of fluids. Dehydration and a bad diet can lead to drowsiness, a shortened attention span and a general feeling of lethargy – not good when you are trying to maintain focus. Try to drink at least a litre and a half of water a day and consume five different pieces of fruit and vegetables. You will feel the benefit instantly.

EXAM BUSTER

THE FASTEST PEN IN THE WEST

You need to be able to write quickly in exams. Practise speed-writing in timed conditions and find a pen that enables you to do so comfortably.

STRESS BEATER

STRESS LEVELS

Stress can build up gradually. Make sure you keep a check on your stress levels and always timetable relaxing activities after long revision sessions.

THE POWER WITHIN

In order to succeed in passing exams
and obtain the best possible result,
you must make a conscious decision
to maximise your potential and create
within yourself resources of will-
power and self-motivation. Once you
have made this decision, you will
need to apply consistent effort
throughout the entire revision
process, and this book will
show you how.

WHAT'S YOUR OBJECTIVE?

Most people will answer this question with something like 'I want to pass', 'I want to get an A' or 'I will be happy just to get through it'. There's nothing necessarily wrong with these objectives, but they will not help you a great deal when taking exams or planning revision. It is more useful to have smaller, more immediate goals, such as: 'For the next twenty minutes I will make notes on Topic X and then I will spend an hour writing up an essay.'

BREAK IT DOWN

These candidates will manage to transfer the intellectual content of their head into that of the examiner with the greatest accuracy. Be sure that each answer you give is really the very best answer, not just one that fills the space.

IT'S ALL ABOUT DISCIPLINE

Good self-discipline is what is going to get you the highest grades. You need to balance your social, family and work commitments so that you remain calm and focused and – most importantly – sane. Bestselling author Anthony Trollope wrote forty novels whilst working full-time as the general manager of a Post Office, by working during office breaks, on trains or at breakfast. With a little effort, you too can be that prolific.

LEAD US NOT INTO TEMPTATION

There will be occasions when you become tempted by activities more appealing than a few hours at the books. These can vary from trips to the pub and shopping excursions, to more inane distractions such as seeing how many times a light switch can be flicked before the bulb blows or even organising your CDs by alphabet and genre. You must be strong – remind yourself why you are doing the exam in the first place.

IDENTIFY YOUR ANXIETIES

Recognition is the first step in dealing with any problem or fear. This applies equally to the exam process. Examine the following statements, be honest with yourself about which apply to you and then tick them accordingly. If necessary, add any others that you think are important in the spaces provided. Revisit these pages regularly to assess your revision progress.

I find it difficult to begin revising ☐
I sleep badly during a revision period ☐
I think I am going to fail ☐
I don't have a revision timetable ☐
I can't stick to my timetable ☐
I can't concentrate on my revision ☐
I forget what I have just learnt ☐
Everyone else is more confident ☐
I don't work hard enough ☐
I don't start revising early enough ☐
Maybe I should give up completely ☐

.... ☐

.... ☐

.... ☐

KNOWLEDGE IS POWER

Your ability to motivate yourself repeatedly to revise will be a key determining factor as to which grade you achieve in any exam you take. However, your level of motivation can be influenced by many external factors – over which you can, in fact, exercise some control. It is important to keep a close check on your mental well-being and allow time for your mind to recover from periods of revision by rewarding it with a variety of different stimuli.

Overcoming your anxieties

I FIND IT DIFFICULT TO BEGIN REVISING

The best way to conquer this problem is to sit down, get your books out and begin. Successful revision depends on self-motivation – nobody can do it for you.

Once you have managed that much, make use of the revision tips featured later in this book and the whole process will become much easier than you think.

I SLEEP BADLY DURING A REVISION PERIOD

Some useful tips to help you sleep when the stress of revision is keeping you awake:

Take a warm bath
Drink warm milk
Get a massage
Ventilate your bedroom
Drink herbal tea
Get up earlier in the morning
Lie with your head facing north
(it works!)

Rub your stomach
Visualise something boring
Visualise something peaceful
Wiggle your toes
Breathe deeply
Don't nap in the daytime
Avoid illuminated clocks
Avoid caffeine
Avoid tobacco
Avoid alcohol

I THINK I AM GOING TO FAIL

Once you have consciously made the decision to pass your exams and have begun some serious revision, you will find that you are able to replace this thought with 'I know I am going to pass.' Doubt usually stems from a guilty conscience.

I DON'T HAVE A
REVISION TIMETABLE

A revision timetable can be one of the most valuable tools available in the run-up to exams. Preparing a timetable creates a visual plan that will show you clearly how you are going to cover all of the topics that need to be included in your revision.

time	m	t	w	t	f	s	s
9							
10							
11							
12							
13							
14							
15							
16							
17							
18							
19							
20							
21							

I CAN'T STICK TO MY TIMETABLE

Most people find revision difficult and often boring, but if you want to achieve good grades then it must be done. Reward yourself on completion of chunks of revision and make sure that your timetable is arranged to suit the times of day that you work best.

I CAN'T CONCENTRATE ON MY REVISION

Many people have difficulty maintaining their attention span over an extended period of time. During revision periods, the problem can be avoided by taking regular breaks, eating and drinking well to keep your energy levels high, breaking your revision up into chunks, working in good lighting conditions (preferably daylight) and making sure your work environment is at a comfortable temperature.

I FORGET WHAT I HAVE JUST LEARNT

If you find yourself staring blankly at your notes or textbooks then take a break or change topics. Your revision plan should provide variation amongst the topics you need to revise; not only from day to day, but preferably hour to hour. There is a reason that schools vary their timetables – people cannot maintain their learning focus on one subject for an extended period of time. By regularly changing revision topic and taking breaks, this problem should be overcome.

EVERYONE ELSE IS MORE CONFIDENT

Take no notice. The people who come across with the most confidence and bravado are normally the people who are actually the most nervous and have done the least amount of study. People behave differently under stressful conditions and exam time is no exception. Concentrate on your own study and make sure that your confidence comes from being satisfied with the amount of effort you have put in.

I DON'T WORK
HARD ENOUGH

You may be feeling this way for one of
two reasons:

1. You have worked yourself up into a state of neurosis and have in fact done more than enough work.

In some cases, the first instance may
be more problematic than the
second. If you feel yourself becoming
neurotic about your revision, then
slow down and take a break because
the chances are that the amount of

information you are absorbing is decreasing rapidly. Successful revision is not about the number of hours you spend revising but about your approach and commitment to a programme of well-planned, regular study.

2. You genuinely haven't done enough work and need to step it up a little.

If you fall into the second category then you really need to work harder.

The best way to determine if you are revising successfully is to create and follow a revision timetable, and to test yourself regularly against past examination papers.

I DON'T START REVISING EARLY ENOUGH

It's time to change your ways. Give yourself a reasonable amount of time to cover all of the topics that may come up in your exams. Regularly return to and retest yourself on previous topics and you will find that you absorb your revision much more efficiently. If you cram your revision into just a few days before each exam you will not achieve a high grade. It is impossible to absorb information at that rate and you will be lucky to retain even ten per cent of what you revise.

MAYBE I SHOULD GIVE UP COMPLETELY

Never. If you are feeling like this then talk to your friends, teachers or parents, or call any of the counselling advice lines offered by most colleges and universities. There are some national advice lines listed at the back of this book. There are people who are trained to help if you are in this state of mind. Don't be embarrassed about asking for assistance or feeling a little low because you certainly won't be the first person to have experienced this.

EXAM BUSTER

SPLISH SPLASH!

Feel revitalised and clean on the day of your exams by having a shower before you leave. It will help to wake you up and enable you to begin the day in a fresh and confident mood.

STRESS BEATER

TIDY UP

Working in messy surroundings often causes a feeling of claustrophobia or anxiety. Keep your revision area clear and tidy.

EXAM BUSTER

THIRSTY WORK

Keep yourself well hydrated in order to help maintain your attention and focus.

EXAM BUSTER

DO THE WRITE THING

Make sure all of your pens work and you have the correct equipment for your exams. Do this the day before in order to make the day of the exam as stress-free as possible. If you need other equipment, such as calculators, check you have spare batteries.

STRESS BEATER

TREAT YOURSELF

Go shopping and treat yourself. Spend some time choosing that new outfit to wear when you are celebrating finishing your exams. If you have been committed in your revision, wearing it will feel that much better.

The revision process examined

WHAT SHOULD I REVISE?

PAST PAPERS

Look at past exam papers as it is usually fairly easy to identify a pattern in topics that have arisen in the past and therefore may arise again.

Discuss your findings with the relevant tutor – they may not be able to help you specifically, but will certainly give you an idea of whether you are moving in the right direction. Past papers are particularly useful for analysing the style and construction of exam questions.

COURSEWORK

Look back over coursework and divide it up into topics or subject headings. Doing this will enable you to spread your revision topics out over a well-planned timetable. If you have taken notes during the course then make sure you have a full set. It can be a useful exercise to check your set of notes with a friend on the same course.

TUTORS

Speaking to a tutor when you begin planning your revision programme is invaluable. Discuss with them what topics you should be revising – it is better to be safe than sorry. And remember; it looks worse on them if you fail so they should be more than willing to help you.

WHEN SHOULD I REVISE?

LIFESTYLE REVIEW

Only you will know when you can work at your optimal level. You must be honest with yourself when deciding this and possibly make some important lifestyle changes. If you work best in the morning but like to sleep in late, then for the duration of the exam period you should consider going to bed earlier so you can get up earlier and maximise the efficiency of your work. When the benefit far outweighs the cost, such lifestyle changes must be made.

PEAK PRACTICE TIME

- Do you prefer to study early in the morning, during the day or late at night?

- During which part of the day have you carried out your strongest work?

- How can you motivate yourself to work at this time every day?

LENGTH OF STUDY PERIODS

The ideal length of each study period can differ from person to person but to find out what works best for you, try varying the amount of time you spend revising at the start of your revision programme. Test yourself to see how well you have absorbed what you have been studying and use the results to decide on a time frame which suits you. A reasonable guideline is to spend 45 minutes to one hour at a time revising.

STAYING ATTENTIVE

Once you have decided on an optimal time frame for each revision session, whereby you are able to consistently maintain your attention, it is important to remember to take regular breaks. Don't just finish an hour of revision in one subject and launch straight into another subject. Stop for ten minutes and let your mind recompose itself between chunks of revision – it will help you absorb your study.

STRESS BEATER

BLAZE THOSE TUNES

As long as it doesn't disrupt your concentration, it's OK to listen to music while you revise. If possible, listen to music without words as they can be quite a distraction when trying to absorb particularly taxing subjects.

WHERE SHOULD I REVISE?

It is generally considered that the best place to revise is the place in which the exam will take place. However, in most cases revising in the exam hall is not possible, so the best thing to do is to vary the location in which you revise, thus creating in your mind a larger variety of accessing cues. For example:

THE LIBRARY

The library can be an excellent place to revise. Here, it is possible to access a wealth of information when you are unsure about certain aspects of your revision. However, libraries can be daunting places and are often full of distractions such as friends and acquaintances. The majority of your revision should be uninterrupted and conducted privately (although group revision can be useful – more on that later).

NO PLACE LIKE HOME

For most people, home is where the majority of revision takes place. Humans are naturally at ease in comfortable and familiar surroundings where they can control the temperature and volume levels, have easy access to food and drink, and can work undisturbed. If you think it would be helpful, give the people you live with a copy of your revision timetable and ask them to respect your need for peace during the times you have allocated for study.

THE GREAT OUTDOORS

Sometimes revising outside can be a refreshing change. Revising in parks, for instance, can be very peaceful. However, be warned – on a windy day your notes may be blown away and you could find yourself spending more time chasing after them than actually revising!

If you do choose this option it is a good idea to move around during your revision, as it will help freshen up your attention levels. When you have a break, try taking a stroll.

EXAM BUSTER

THE EARLY BIRD FINDS HIS OR HER SEAT

If you need to find out where you are sitting in the exam hall then give yourself time to do so, even if it means getting up a little bit earlier.

STRESS BEATER

KEEP FIT

Healthy body, healthy mind. If you look after your physical well-being then your mind will be sharper and more active and you will absorb your revision much more efficiently.

CARRY A NOTEBOOK

This will help you to make the most of those small pockets of 'free' time, such as standing in bus queues, waiting for trains or walking from place to place. If you were able to learn three mathematical equations per day by doing this, then over a month you would have learnt... ninety new equations.

Revision techniques

BE ACTIVE

The most important point to remember when revising is that any revision you do must be active. Simply reading and rereading your notes is a passive approach and you will retain far less information than if you used active revision techniques. Furthermore, active revision is far more likely to be enjoyable, and this is important if you want to maximise the amount of information you take in.

DIAGRAMS AND TABLES

Draw diagrams and pictures and make tables of your information. They will be much easier to remember and are easier to distinguish in your mind than pages of similar looking notation.

MIND MAPPING

Also known as spider diagrams or brainstorms, these are excellent visual representations of the way that the brain deals with information. Try writing down a subject heading in the middle of the page and then add branches to structure the detail of your revision.

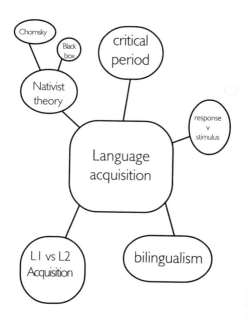

Chomsky

Black box

Nativist theory

critical period

response v stimulus

Language acquisition

L1 vs L2 Acquisition

bilingualism

EXAM BUSTER

PRIME TIME

If you can't remember a fact or a name, try singing to yourself, doodling or even writing down the entire alphabet – it may be just the trigger you need.

MNEMONICS

Mnemonics are a good way of remembering important phrases or quotes by using abbreviations, words or rhyming phrases. An example of this is a common method of teaching the fates of Henry VIII's six wives:

Divorced, beheaded, died
divorced, beheaded, survived

REVISING WITH OTHERS

Group revision sessions are helpful opportunities to discuss any doubts or uncertainties you have about any subject matter you are revising. Often a light discussion will clear up any misunderstanding of a topic that you might have and can also be valuable practice in how to approach structuring an essay on that topic. This type of revision session should not, however, feature too heavily in your revision programme as distractions can prove more difficult to resist when tin a group.

REWARDS

Reward yourself on completion of a successful day's or week's revision. It can boost morale and provide welcome relief from studying. Even eating a nice meal or having a social drink can be a good reward.

EXAM BUSTER

NO TALKING!

Avoid talking about the exam subject on the morning of the exam – it will only make you stressed. Somebody is bound to mention a topic you are not feeling confident about and it will not help your peace of mind.

STRESS BEATER

GET A MASSAGE

Most sports centres offer massage services, often with discounted rates for students. There is nothing better to help you unwind from a period of sustained revision than a really vigorous massage. You will feel more relaxed afterwards in both body and mind.

The exam

THE NIGHT BEFORE

Pack your bag. Check and recheck that you have all the equipment necessary to sit your exam. Check that your pens work and take back-ups and a pencil. If you are using a calculator, there is no harm in replacing the batteries as part of your preparation. Also remember to pack any drink or sweets that you wish to take.

EXAM BUSTER

READ IT LOUD AND CLEAR

Read the question carefully – in fact, read it twice – and make sure that you answer the question that is written on the paper, even if it is not quite what you have prepared for.

STRESS BEATER

SHARE THE WORKLOAD

Meet up with friends to discuss any issues that have arisen in your revision, or anxieties in your life. A problem shared is a problem halved, and an exam period is no time to be sitting on problems.

ALARM BELLS

Make sure that you have a back-up alarm. It is probably unlikely that your alarm clock will fail, but if the mobile phone battery runs out or you have a power cut in the night, you could be in trouble. It's better to be prepared for all eventualities and the security in knowing you have a reserve wake-up call could aid a better night's sleep.

GET UP EARLY

For many people this may not be a problem, as the night before an exam may be a sleepless one. For those of you who have no trouble sleeping in, whatever the day has in store, remember that it is not every day that you have something as important as an exam to prepare yourself for. Having enough time to compose yourself and get ready slowly will help to keep you calm and maintain your focus.

THE BUS IS LATE

Take an early bus. Many establishments have strict policies about arriving late for exams and most will not let you sit the exam if your lateness stretches beyond a certain period – sometimes this is simply once the exam has begun.

OUTSIDE THE EXAMINATION ROOM

Right outside the exam room can be a horrendous place to spend the final minutes before you sit an exam. Inevitably there will be people brimming with confidence who may throw you off your stride by claiming to have revised everything possible and thus begin to plant seeds of doubt in your mind. Ignore these people by focusing inwardly on remaining calm and composed.

EXAM BUSTER

NO PEEKING!

Looking around to see what your friends are doing in an exam hall will only serve to distract them and you. If everybody else is working then it generally means you should be too.

STRESS BEATER

VEG OUT

There is no point revising all day every day as your brain will overload and your revision will become inefficient. Give yourself time to lie on the sofa and switch off. Watch your favourite soaps or turn on that PlayStation and hammer those buttons.

DON'T REREAD YOUR NOTES

If you have successfully stuck to a well-planned revision schedule then you should not really be rereading any revision notes before you enter an exam. The time is better spent focusing your mind and trying to remain calm. You may also find that rereading your notes causes you to feel tense, especially if you read something you are unsure of. It is too late to learn anything new at this point.

THE EXAM ROOM

Now you will see if the revision you have done has paid off. If you have stuck to your revision schedule you should find yourself feeling composed and confident, although, of course, some people will still be feeling highly nervous. Just try to find your seat, sit down, focus your mind and avoid talking to anyone else or looking around.

LISTEN TO THE INSTRUCTIONS

It is really important to pay attention to the instructions given at the start of any exam. Invigilators may be divulging some important last minute information. There may be issues raised on entering candidate numbers or course codes etc. All of your hard work could be in vain if the examiners cannot correctly identify you by the details you provide.

ANSWER THE QUESTIONS

The questions may not be structured exactly as you would like, but you must make sure you answer what is asked of you and not what you would like to be asked. There is no point writing everything you know about a certain topic just to demonstrate the amount of information you have learnt. You will be marked higher for using only the relevant information.

WRITE LEGIBLY

Take your time and make sure that your handwriting and presentation is clear. Examiners cannot award marks for something they cannot read, no matter how good a point you make.

EXAM BUSTER

PUT PEN TO PAPER

The most difficult hurdle in any exam is writing the first few words, whether it's for a short answer question or an essay question. It is better to write something and correct it than to spend ages thinking about the perfect introduction.

STRESS BEATER

GO OUT ON THE TOWN

Remember you are not alone in having to revise. Reward yourself and your friends with some fun and relaxation at the end of a sustained period of revision. This period should be measured in days – not hours!

ASK FOR HELP

If you really don't understand what a particular question is getting at, do ask the examiner. They may not be allowed or even able to help you, but it certainly won't hurt to ask.

STRESS BEATER

TALK, TALK, TALK

If you have concerns, or are feeling anxious about any aspect of your revision or exam taking, it is a good idea to talk about it. Discussing your problems with friends, family and teachers is a good way to relieve some of that tension.

CLEAR IT UP

When you are writing your answers and later checking what you have written, always check the clarity of your work. Examiners do not have time to interpret any ambiguities in your work or fathom your intentions. For instance, if you are referring to multiple sources in your work, make sure you identify each clearly.

DON'T PANIC

If you find yourself getting agitated, fidgeting or hyperventilating, then put down your pen, have a drink of water, close your eyes and relax for a few moments. It is more productive to rest for a while and resume work in a calm and assured manner than to try to get some coherent thoughts down on paper whilst feeling wound up.

HALF A MARK IS BETTER THAN NO MARK

Make sure you try to write something for every question or problem in the exam. It is better to attempt an answer and achieve a partial credit than to leave a blank space in the hope of making marks up on other questions. Examiners will look more favourably on you if you have at least attempted to answer every question.

EXAM BUSTER

PLAN FOR POINTS

If you run out of time, writing rough plans for answers to any remaining questions may gain you valuable marks.

EXAM BUSTER

TIME MANAGEMENT

When in the exam, divide up the available time appropriately, leaving more time to spend on questions with more marks allocated to them. It may seem obvious, but candidates frequently forget this important step.

DON'T REPEAT – THAT IS, DON'T REPEAT

When answering the questions, there is no need to repeat the exact wording of the question you have been asked. The examiner knows what the question is and will not appreciate having to reread it on each student's paper. Be careful, also, not to make the same point simply using slightly different wording. You must be concise in your responses. If the question requires a one-word answer, then that is what you must give.

SHOW YOUR WORKINGS

If you are doing calculations, make it absolutely clear to the examiner how you arrived at the answer. The right answer is often only a small percentage of your mark and it is the working out that carries the most weighting. However, don't camouflage your page with scribbles, arrows and crossings out – you are usually allowed extra sheets for working out. Take advantage of these and make your work on the exam paper easily decipherable.

USE THE RIGHT PEN

Fight the temptation to use red or green ink in your work. It may seem clearer, but spare a thought for the examiner. It will be quite infuriating for them if you present your work in the colour with which they wish to mark it. Exam boards usually stipulate which colours and even types of pen are acceptable, so be sure to find this out prior to the exam.

HAND IN ON TIME

Nothing will rile an invigilator or examiner more than if they have to wrestle you for your exam paper, so try to make sure you really do put your pen down as soon as the allocated time is up. You don't want to risk being penalised for failing to adhere to this rule.

After the exam

IT'S ALL OVER

Don't waste time mulling over what could have been. If you have revised thoroughly, the chances are that your results will reflect this. It is either time to go out and celebrate in any way you deem appropriate or, if you have more exams, forget about the previous and concentrate on excelling in the next one.

DON'T DISCUSS IT

Getting involved in discussing what your peers have written or how they answered questions can only sow seeds of doubt in your mind. It can make you feel vulnerable and inadequate. No two people will have answered questions in exactly the same way, so the safest thing to do is to avoid talking about it and instead discuss which pub to go to.

Why people fail

YOU WEREN'T BORN READY

Some people take exams hoping for a fluke. They hope that they have learnt enough by simply doing the coursework and attending lectures. This will ultimately result in under-achieving or failure. Don't be one of these people – be prepared for your exams.

ONE OR TWO TOPICS IS NEVER ENOUGH

You are unlikely to achieve your best result in an exam if you simply revise one or two of the topics in the syllabus and hope that they are included in the exam. Success depends on thorough revision and studying a broad spectrum of topics. Often revising a greater cross-section of topics will help you with areas that you have difficulties with.

THE PRESSURE IS BUILDING

During an exam period, people often spend more time reflecting upon the implications that passing or failing a course will have on the rest of their lives. However, this isn't always productive. If the exam is crucial to qualify in a chosen career, or in moving on to the next level of education in a chosen institution, the added pressure can often distract from the need to knuckle down and study.

Put things into perspective – if you've worked hard there's no reason why you should fail and every reason why you should pass. Remind yourself that in the unlikely event that you do fail, there are worse disasters in the world.

NEVER BE TOO CONFIDENT

Overconfidence breeds complacency. This is a dangerous mentality to adopt and can lead to disappointment on results day. You can never be too prepared for an exam and often a sense of overconfidence is disguising a lack of good preparation.

STICKING TO THE TIMETABLE

It is impossible to stress enough that a successful revision programme depends on sticking to a revision timetable. Don't become one of those people who cannot stop revising a subject until they are a world authority on it. A balance of subject matter, combined with a sensible structure of relaxation and study, is vital.

THE GLASS IS HALF EMPTY

Pessimism breeds laziness. Don't fall into the mindset that you are definitely going to fail. It will decrease your motivation and attention when you really need to be revising. If you are having these thoughts then the chances are you need to do a bit more work than most – don't let this scare you. Exams are designed to be passed and there is no reason why you shouldn't manage.

STRESS BEATER

READ – FOR FUN!

It may be the last thing you want to do, but don't forget how rewarding it can be to read a book solely for pleasure. Lose yourself in the fantastical pages of a great novel or in the faraway lands of an exciting travel memoir.

EXAM BUSTER

CHECK AND RECHECK

Once you have finished an exam, do reread and recheck your work. Examiners appreciate fluency and coherence in answer structure and this can only be gauged by reading what you have written in its entirety. Allow time at the end to do this if possible.

STRESS BEATER

EAT MORE CHOCOLATE

Chocolate has a high sugar content and is a good way to boost your energy levels when your enthusiasm for revision is waning.

STRESS BEATER

CATCH A FILM

There is nothing like a good movie to take your mind off the books. Venture out to the cinema and distance yourself from your revision space. This will enable you to have a really clean break from studying and return with a much clearer mind.

Good luck!

Whether you agree with it or not, exam-taking is a fundamental part of education and being well prepared for taking them is of massive importance. Start early, spread out your workload and try to stay relaxed during the whole process. A bit of careful planning goes a long way, and if you are methodical and organised you will find the whole process much easier.

Good luck!

The Student Counselling Service
Visit their website to find the contact
details for your college:
www.studentcounselling.org

The Samaritans
Telephone: 08457 909090 or visit
their website: www.samaritans.org

ChildLine
Younger exam takers can call
ChildLine on 0800 1111 or visit their
website: www.childline.org.uk

Also from Summersdale

DRIVING TEST TIPS

summersdale *self-help*

DRIVING TEST TIPS
ISBN 1 84024 389 9
£2.50 P/b

Don't let preparing for your driving test drive you up the wall!

With tips from instructors and new drivers alike for both before and during the exam, this little book is jam-packed with helpful advice to make sure that you feel in fine form for the open road… and that you lose your L-plates and not your cool.

De-stress for
EXAMS

summersdale *self-help*

DE-STRESS FOR EXAMS
ISBN 1 84024 390 2
£2.50 P/b

You may have 101 textbooks about your chosen subject, but this is the only one you'll ever need on how to de-stress for your exams.

Coping with stress while taking exams can be more testing than the papers themselves. *De-stress for Exams* will ensure you enter that exam hall with a clear head and a calm attitude – essential for tackling tests with the best possible chance of success.

Rosie Hamilton-McGinty

A Winning Attitude

TO CHANGE YOUR LIFE – CHANGE YOUR ATTITUDE

A WINNING ATTITUDE

Rosie Hamilton-McGinty

ISBN 1 84024 404 6

£2.99 P/b

'… this little book could give you a whole new outlook on life.'

Brighton Evening Argus

With a winning attitude, you can: motivate and guide yourself; do right by others; open the way to empathy; become caring and compassionate.

www.summersdale.com